RIDDLES FOR CHILDREN

BY ARMAND COALLIER

"Riddles for Children," by Armand Coallier. ISBN 1-58939-683-9 (softcover).

Library of Congress Control Number on file with Publisher.

Published 2004 by Virtualbookworm.com Publishing Inc., P.O. Box 9949, College Station, TX 77845, US.

Manufactured in the United States of America.

Acknowledgments

My deepest appreciation to my wife Louise for her help and patience while I worked on this project.

A very special "Thank You" to all the children who ride my school bus. Their input as they read and amused themselves with draft copies of this work was extremely helpful. I can say with absolute honesty that this work has been field-tested. And that it has proved to be an effective tool in helping to educate children while keeping them occupied and challenged intellectually.

And finally I would like to thank Bill Gates for without Windows® this work would have been virtually impossible.

*"I have never seen an ugly smile nor
a pretty frown."*

Armand Coallier

To my wife Louise, my children; Tina, Donna, and Steve and to my granddaughter, Rachel, whose love and support has made so many of my dreams come true and…

to Gracie; an angel who touched my heart for but a few short moments yet changed my life forever.

Put on your thinking caps and lets go...

What's on the bottom and is needed for a change?
A diaper.

What do you have at home that always runs out but never leaves?

Time

What kind of shoes does a presidential candidate wear?

Running shoes

What kind of hit makes a good dinner?
A chop

What kind of mail can a mouse send?
An e-mail

What can you have on your hands that is completely weightless?

Time

What kind of professional can help you board a ship?
A Doc

What kind of food can help us smile?

Cheese

What does everyone have that can be good or bad?
Habits

What do you go on every day that takes you to all sorts of places?
On foot

What can you swing without moving?
Your mood

What cools you on a hot summer day and is a snap?

A breeze

What do you miss when you're being bad?
You misbehave.

Where can you buy stars?
At a general store

What kind of frame usually has a scene in it but not a photo?
A window frame

What do peas and whales have in common?
They both hang around in pods.

What can you hit that will take you down?

The slopes

What will kill you if you bite it?
The dust

What can you charge but can't pay cash for?
A dead battery

Why are elephants always ready for a swim?

Because they always have their trunks on.

What can be your date but can't take you to the movies?

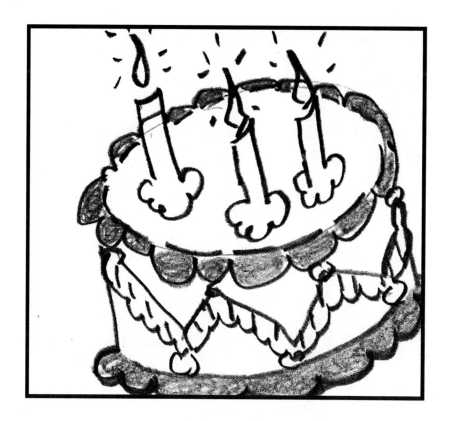

Your birthday

What's a real safe place?
A bank

What does a motel, a river, and your home have in common?
They all have beds.

What can you download and use to fix your nails?
A file

Where's the best place to find lots of ghosts?
A Ghost Town

What kind of room can you find in cyberspace?

A chat room

What do you call the corner of a diamond?
A base

What kind of mat keeps you looking fresh?
A Laundromat

What keeps you safe & your hair neat?
A net

What do you call supporters of the arts?

Easels

What do you call an old card player?

An antique dealer

What part of your foot can be fun to play with?
The ball

How does time travel?

It flies

Where is it OK to find flies?
On pants

What's the nosiest bird?

An owl (always saying "who?")

What part of a cake can make an egg?
A layer (a chicken)

Why do chickens refuse to fly?

Because they like to lay around.

What relatives do you hate to see at your family picnic?
Ants

What kind of business can be really amusing?

Show business

What do you call the first lady's garden?
Garden of Eden

What kind of meat can slay a vampire?

A stake

What part of a boat is the cheapest to shop for?
A sail

What can you gather without lifting a finger?

Dust

Why does your nose run?
To stay in front of your face

What kind of water is always leaking?

Holy water

What do corduroy pants and a Zebra have in common?
Stripes

Where do you find the smartest insects?

At a spelling bee

What kind of meat is hard to swallow?
Bologna

What two things can you get paid for practicing?

Law and medicine

What letter can you ride if you add tax to it first?
The letter "C" (Tax C – taxi)

What kind of party can give you a headache?

A bash

Why would you cry over a leek?
Because it's an onion

What kind of flower has more than one lip?

A tulip

What kind of tomato speaks a foreign tongue?
An Italian tomato

What kind of animal gathers information?

A mole

What kind of drink did we name a party after?
Tea

What is it that sometimes sits by your bed, is sometimes read, can be little and black?

A book

What kind of steel does Tiger like to use.
Irons

What can a bottle do with a tie?

Wear it around its neck

If you are going to get dressed properly what should you put into your shoes first?
Your toes

✳ Where are you if you can only go south?

At the North Pole

Where does Santa keep his suit?
In his Claus closet

What's evil and walks in water?

Darth Wader

Why did the railroad cars go off the track?
They were untrained

What can put the squeeze on you all day long but you'll never give it a dime?

A boa

What comes before a T-top?
An "Estop" (S-top)

What kind of dance requires mowing the lawn?

Hula (Grass skirt dance)

What's the best way to draw a picture on your PC?
Bit-by-bit

Where does a three hundred pound gorilla sleep?

Wherever he wants

How do you eat piecemeal?
Bit by bit

What time of the year are boxers the busiest?

During the holidays (Boxing gifts)

What can you stand on, and breathe into your lungs?
Water (As ice and steam)

What kind of animal can cause a leak?

A rat

What can run downhill, never uphill and can never walk anywhere?
Water

If you had three feet what would you be?

A yard

What should you stick with during good and bad times?
Glue

What kind of sport equipment can fly?

A bat

Why is giving up like a bear's winter home?
Because it's a cave inn

What kind of crab loves Halloween?

Ghost crab

Why is a touchdown music to the coach's ear?
Because it's a score

Where do spiders shop for food?

On the web

What does a man have that leaves you with a message when reversed?
Male voice (Voice Mail)

Why did the witch make her cat talk?

Because she wanted to hear his tale.

What happens when the ghoul burns up?
He becomes goulash.

What kind of planet would leave the dinner table?

A full moon

What sort of bell can fill you up?
Taco Bell

Where would you go to find first graders or fish?

A School

What can run on legs but can't walk?
Stockings

What part of a lion is really hairy?

The mane part

How are elephants and skunks similar?
Neither can be ignored if they're in the living room.

45

What can babies do grownups can't?

Celebrate their first birthday

How often do you celebrate your first birthday?
Once a year

Why was Eve punished for taking an apple?

Because it was in Eden's garden.

Where does a skunk sit in church?
In the pew

47

What's a mess and no cost to anyone?
A free for all

What kind of demon loves to take chances?

A daredevil

What can you charge and not approach?
A fee

What kind of role doesn't require good acting?

A dinner roll

What can you put on every day and not grow heavier?
Airs

✳ What works better when it's retired?

A car

In what building can you find a ruler?
The White House

What kind of toy can you fit an elephant under?

A big top

What beverage do golfers have before every hole?
Tea

What part of a coat can you take out to sea?

A liner

Why do people leave after eating?
Because they're fed up.

What kind of female is not quite right?

A miss

What kind of cookie can make you lose your temper?
A snap

How do you eliminate a shadow?

Shave

What kind of shake is loved by everyone?
A fair shake

What can bring you flowers or move you?

A van

Name a country that can be bought by any one any time?
Turkey

What do you find in a box that can help you fix a flat?

A jack

What kind of egg is best for older people?
A nest egg

In what air force was president Clinton?

Air Force One

What can you make shorter by taking it up?
A dress

What kind of dreams do plumbers have?

Pipe dreams

What do boy scouts have in common with a good meal?
They're both prepared

Why did Adam have to go to the super market for his vegetables?

Because he was banned from the garden.

Why is a window sometimes like a big fat fabrication?
Because they both can be shaded.

What kind of doughnut can be flown?

A plane doughnut

What kind of noodles can you find inside your sweater everyday?
Elbows

What letter, when colored red, can be sailed upon?

"C" (The red sea)

Where can you go surfing but not swimming?
Ebay

What kind of roll can you nap on?

A bed roll

What kind of race is never won?
The human race

What's the best place to get rich quick?

At the bakery where you can get a lot of dough.

Why are laptops like babies?
They can both sit on your lap.

What kind of grapes can fly?

Concords

What can you add to aid that could get you in trouble?
A bet (Aid and abet)

What spirit was the first to reach across the ocean without sailing?

The Spirit of St. Louis

What kinds of cats are used for transportation?
Cougars and Jaguars

What looks better after they're crunched?

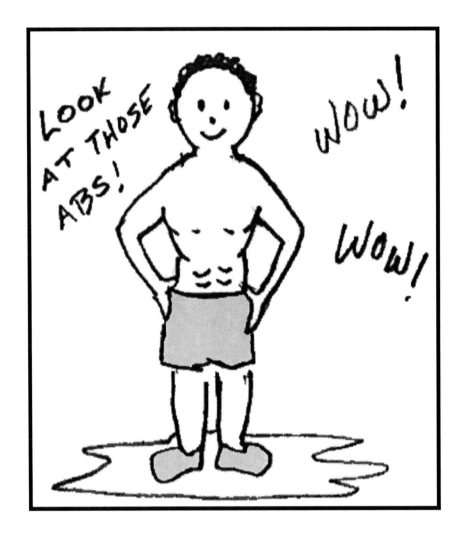

Abs

What does a prison have in common with your body?
They both have cells.

What kind of fit takes more than one person?

An outfit

Why are homerun hitters never in danger?
Because they are always safe

What country can help the wheels on the bus turn better?

Greece

What can you throw that always upsets everyone around you?
A tantrum

What the darkest part of a king's army?

The knights

What kind of tissue will never give you ring around the collar?
Clean necks (Kleenex)

What kind of container follows <u>you</u> and can help you do almost anything?

A can (You can)

What kind of number can hurt you?
A pin number

What kind of number can help you get some cash?

A pin number

What can you have in your pocket that can costs you a lot of money?
A hole

What baked goodies can you eat as much of as you want and never get fat?

Doughnut holes

What can be read like a newspaper or red like an apple?
Lips

What kind of squash can grow a tree?

Acorn

What kind of dope can be of great value?
Inside dope

What disappears when you pack it away?

Food

What's the only way to start vacation?
With a "V"

What do saints and cars have in common?

Headlights

What kind of ship makes the best meal?
A sub

What type of office machine could help you win a battle?

A Cannon

What kind of stick can help you find answers?
A cue stick

What kind of vehicle should you ride to be better fit?

Train

What is dangerous to peddle in the middle of the street?
Drugs

What do a fairy and your dog have in common?

A tale

What's the best place to see a lot of dashes?
A track meet

What kind of table can accommodate any number?

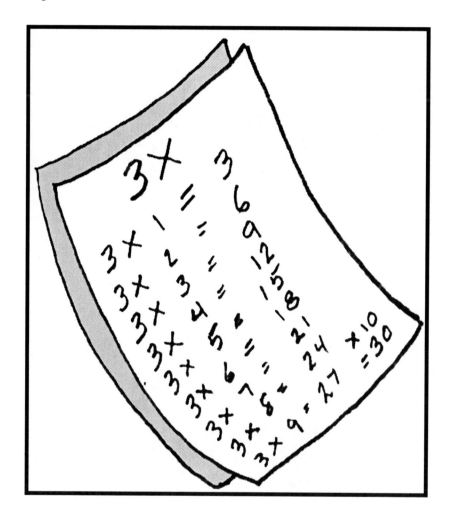

A times table

What kind of emperor can make a good meal?
A Caesar

What kind of sport equipment is the loudest?

A racket

If you appear, or run down someone's pant leg, what could you be?
A seam (seem to be)

What can you burn by stepping on it?

Gas

What kind of points cannot be scored?
Viewpoints

Why are cats confused about whom to obey?

Because they have four paws (fathers).

What's the first lady's name?
Eve

What kind of elevation takes years away?

A face lift

What's the saddest color?
Blue

When is it OK to put jelly in you front door?

When it's ajar

What kind of furniture sounds nice?
A musical chair

Why did the skeleton run away from the dog?

Because dogs love to chew on bones

What do cups have in common with your face?
Lips

What's the best way to back up good friends?

Put them in reverse

Why is an easy chair like a teddy bear?
Because it's stuffed

What part of a group can get you ready for a race?

A set (Get "ready," "set," go....)

Why is a barber always ahead?
Because he knows the short cuts.

What kind of old sailor can you use to make a road?

Tar

What can you add to your mail to make it lighter?
The letter "E" (E-mail)

What kind of food is good for your brain?

Food for thought

What kind of story will "NOT" help you make friends?
A tattle tale

What do Ray and Jay do all the time?

Rhyme

What's the best kind of candy to take on a cruise?
Lifesavers

What can you hit that would make you smarter?

The books

What can you do with fat that can help you make friends?
Chew the fat

What's in front of the tee?

"S"

What's heavy and large enough to hold a house?
A lot

What do strikes and schools have in common?

They both have zones.

What kind of stack helps us breathe easier?
A smokestack

If Lincoln were alive today, where would he live?

In a Lego cabin

What do you have to learn to become a good cowboy?
The ropes

What part of a bird do mom and dad not like to get in the mail?

A bill

Why did the reindeer get together at the convention?
Because they wanted to be herd

At what time is it best to knock the king's guard off balance?

Midnight

What kind of dog can help you lose weight?
A holloweenie

What can you go into very deep and at the same time see more clearly?

Thought

Why are we always waiting for Caesar?
Because Caesar is always dressing.

What sort of yelling can be cold and delicious?

I scream

What kind of tots can get you all wet?
Little squirts

What kind of old friend can burn you?

An old flame

When is it possible to throw light?
Whenever you toss lightly

What kind of deceiving game do turtles and oysters play?

Shell games

What does a parking area have in common with a ton of stuff?
They're both a lot

Why is a newspaper like a marching band?

They both have columns

What's the easiest way to find bacon?
Do a strip search

What kind of garment is very sad to receive?

A pink slip

What kind of offspring can be dangerous?
A son of a gun

Where can you drop a heavy wrench on a steel floor and not make a sound?

In space

What's a good place to read or meet a lion?
A den

What part of your family is best at carrying messages?

The males

What part of your shoe can you find at a fish fry?
A sole

What parts of your body can help you build a house?

Nails

What kind of citizen is always welcomed?
A Czech (A check)

What kind of tree has no leaves and never grows?

A clothes tree

What can be a pleasure to use or a very pressing tool?
An Iron

What country can you serve at a cookout?

Chile

Why is a lumber jack like the king of diamonds?
Because they both have axes

In what plant can you find your entire family?

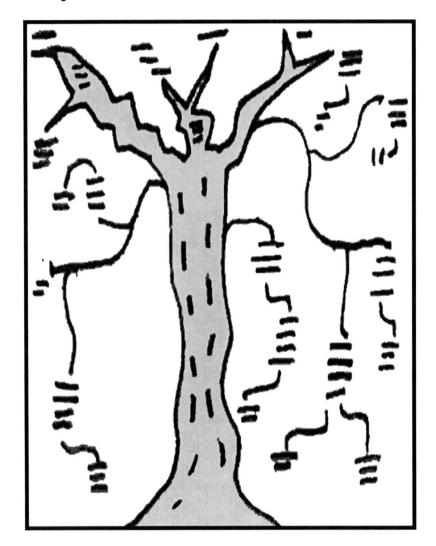

In a family tree

Why is a golf course like a highway?
Because you can drive on both

Why are motor scooters and a golfers alike?

Because they're both putt-putters.

Which of your relatives can you always find at the beach?
Ants

Why do cats chase their tails?

Because they want to hear the end of the tale.

What can you make using no materials?
Time

About the Author

Retired and driving a school bus, Armand Coallier has a passion for his work that he readily shares with anyone willing to listen. Armand's career in advertising has taken him down some interesting paths. As owner and operator of a number of businesses in the Graphic Arts industry, Armand worked his way to Vice President of Western Ag Publishing Company of California. Venturing out on his own, he then conceptualized and launched The American Food and Ag Exporter magazine, an international publication.

When asked, "What has been your secret to success?" Armand has always answered "listen to the needs of others and service them, service, them, service them!." A motto that serves him well in his retirement career. Armand is quick to remind us that serving others is the real key to finding purpose and happiness in our lives.

Lightning Source UK Ltd.
Milton Keynes UK
07 June 2010

155241UK00001B/81/A

9 781589 396838